THE

On Sylvia Plath and Taylor Swift

MAGGIE NELSON

FERN
PRESS

1 3 5 7 9 10 8 6 4 2

Fern Press, an imprint of Vintage, is part of the
Penguin Random House group of companies

Vintage, Penguin Random House UK, One Embassy Gardens,
8 Viaduct Gardens, London SW11 7BW

penguin.co.uk/vintage
global.penguinrandomhouse.com

Penguin
Random House
UK

First published by Fern Press in 2025
Originally published as a limited-edition zine by
Dopazine/Dopamine Books in 2024

Copyright © Maggie Nelson 2025

The moral right of the author has been asserted

No part of this book may be used or reproduced in any manner for the
purpose of training artificial intelligence technologies or systems. In accordance
with Article 4(3) of the DSM Directive 2019/790, Penguin Random House
expressly reserves this work from the text and data mining exception.

Typeset in 11.51/16.45pt Adobe Caslon Pro by
Six Red Marbles UK, Thetford, Norfolk

Printed and bound in Great Britain by Clays Ltd, Elcograf S.p.A.

The authorised representative in the EEA is Penguin Random House Ireland,
Morrison Chambers, 32 Nassau Street, Dublin D02 YH68

A CIP catalogue record for this book is available from the British Library

ISBN 9781911717652

Penguin Random House is committed to a sustainable future
for our business, our readers and our planet. This book is made
from Forest Stewardship Council® certified paper.

MIX
Paper | Supporting
responsible forestry
FSC® C018179
www.fsc.org

for Alba

THE SLICKS

'Above all things, Sylvia Plath desired fame,' Jacqueline Rose tells us in *The Haunting of Sylvia Plath*. 'As [Plath] put it at one point in her *Journals*: "it is sad only to be able to mouth other poets; I want someone to mouth me."'

People did come to mouth Plath, likely more than she could have ever imagined. But the fame came – famously – with and after death. She did not live, for better or worse, to bear the burden of what Rose aptly terms 'the perverse component (voyeurism and sadism) of public acclaim'.

At least in a limited sense, this may have been for the better, insofar as the voyeurism and sadism that have come Plath's way over the past six decades has been fierce and unyielding. (I'm thinking of the shockingly sexist estimations of her work by male critics in the wake of her death; successive feminist battles over whether to venerate or revile her; the punitive management of her literary estate; the spiteful, micromanaged biographies; lawsuits having to do with *The Bell Jar*; the repetitive vandalism of her grave by fans who aimed to chisel 'Hughes' off her name; and, perhaps most violent of all, the reduction of her staggeringly complex body of work into the meme of a sad, mean white girl who died with her head in an oven while her children slept nearby.) As Rose says of Plath's ghost, 'What she may be asking for is never clear, although it seems highly unlikely that she is asking for what she gets.'

Plath didn't live to inhabit her fame, but her work sketches its contours nonetheless. Her poems offer a shrewd guide to the voyeurism and sadism, idolatry and demonisation, which characterise our treatment of the famous, especially famous women – and especially those women who traffic in making the personal public, however mediated or aestheticised. Plath knew all about the 'peanut-crunching crowd [who] / Shoves in to see ... The big strip tease' – an exhibition she explicitly links to money: 'there is a charge, a very large charge / For a word or a touch / Or a bit of blood / Or a piece of my hair or my clothes' ('Lady Lazarus').

Plath was broke when she wrote these lines: no one was paying her much for her writing, much less for a bit of her clothes. But unlike, say, Emily Dickinson – another poet who theorised fame without living it – Plath desperately wanted to be known, acclaimed and paid. She knew – and, more scandalously still, she gave full expression to – the thunderous force of her ambition: she had conviction of her genius, a fierce desire to manifest it, and a drive for others to receive the transmission. Her aspirations were colossal: in fact, the one book of poems Plath published in her lifetime was titled *The Colossus*. In the title poem, the speaker is trying to glue back together the pieces of a giant statue she addresses as 'father' and describes as 'some god or other'; the speaker figures herself as Lilliputian, taking cover at night in the colossus's left ear. But don't be fooled: in puzzling together the statue – and, more crucially, in writing the poem – Plath places herself in the position of creator, even creator of the Creator. 'I think I would like to call myself "The girl who wanted to be God",' she wrote in her *Journals*.

As someone who has spent a lot of time reading and thinking about Plath, and as someone who has also spent a lot of time listening to and thinking about Taylor Swift – whose lyrics and self-presentation, as many have noted, make nods to Plath – I find myself thinking often about the two together. This has been especially so since the April 2024 release of Swift's *The Tortured Poets Department*, as Plath's name has served, for decades now, as a metonym for the tortured poet. (Swift's video for 'Fortnight', the first track on *TTPD*, explicitly merges Plath and Dickinson iconography: Swift appears institutionalised and undergoes crude electric shock while dressed in nineteenth-century Dickinsonian garb.) Plath also serves as a metonym – as does Swift – for a woman who makes art about a broken heart. 'When you give someone your whole heart and he doesn't want it, you cannot take it back,' Plath allegedly told a friend during her brutalising break-up with Ted Hughes. 'It's gone forever.'

When I think about Swift and Plath together, I find myself returning to a simple thought: *Sylvia Plath is dead, and Taylor Swift is alive.* Not only is Swift alive, but she is living in front of us, for us, with us. Some may express incredulity or irritation at the repetitiveness of Swift's paeans to falling in love and subsequent heartache, but when placed beside the severity of Plath's 'it's gone forever', the repetitiveness can be quite heartening, even comic relief. What goes on forever, in Swift, is giving your whole heart, feeling or fearing that it will never come back, then having it return, maybe even despite itself, then being foolish enough to do it all over again (and again, and again). Plath didn't get the chance to ride out this cycle; she ended her life at age thirty. As I write, Swift is thirty-four, and showing no signs of bowing out.

In part because Plath died by suicide, and in part because she left behind (literally, on her desk) an extraordinary, extreme book of poetry, *Ariel*, she posthumously became, in Rose's words, 'a figure for death. Death in the shape of a woman, femininity as deadly.' Swift, by contrast, is no such thing. In fact, one of the words most often associated with Swift's music is 'joy'; Plath, not so much (which is to say, not at all). Swift's fame, and the pleasure of her music, indeed rests in large part on how people experience her as a figure for life, even if that life sometimes involves big feelings that make one 'want to die' ('All Too Well'). This desire appears to be primarily rhetorical, by which I mean only that, so far as we know,

Swift does not have the backstory of serious mental illness such that truly tortured Plath, leading to Plath's unsuccessful suicide attempt at age twenty, and her successful one a decade later. And while Swift plays at menace – most recently (and most convincingly) in *TTPD*'s 'Who's Afraid of Little Old Me?' (to which she answers, 'You should be'), such lines still don't carry the chill of Plath's 'Out of the ash / I rise with my red hair / And I eat men like air' ('Lady Lazarus'). Nor does Swift's work bear, as Plath's infamously does, traces of some of the worst historical catastrophes on record – namely, the Holocaust, with its incinerating violence, and its chaotic landscape of victims, perpetrators, collaborators and bystanders. Writing may have kept Plath alive, but her poems don't shrink from aligning art with death: 'Dying / Is an art, like everything else. / I do it exceptionally well. / I do it so it feels like hell' ('Lady Lazarus'). When Swift visits related territory, the bottom is considerably higher: 'I cry a lot but I am so productive, it's an art' ('I Can Do It With a Broken Heart').

These differences are accidents of fate, personality, epoch and medium; it is not a moral contest. I celebrate Swift's genius for pop, her apparent sanity and joy-giving capacity, her ability to feel and express a wide range of positive and negative emotions without circling the drain, and her transmutation of her emotional life into epic, public journey; I also celebrate Plath's darkness, her outrageous jostling with historical trauma, and her genuinely scary extremity – an extremity I respect even if I wish that she had gotten better care, lived more life, and had the chance to write more things.

Such differences, however, have not kept critics from relying on a remarkably similar script in response to both artists, likely because it's the same script that has greeted female profusion, personalism and ambition literally for millennia. This script – which at this point I could write in my sleep – was on full display in the immediate wake of the release of *TTPD*: rote shaming of making the personal public; calls for the artist to look outside herself for subject matter; charges of her vulnerability being faux, or deployed as manipulative marketing tool; tongue-clucks about self-indulgence and being 'in need of an editor'. Taking the bait of the album's title, the *New York Times* review made its case against Swift's profusion by comparing her to – of all people – Plath, here put to service as disciplinarian to Swift's jouissance:

Sylvia Plath once called poetry 'a tyrannical discipline,' because the poet must 'go so far and so fast in such a small space; you've got to burn away all the peripherals.' Great poets know how to condense, or at least how to edit. The sharpest moments of 'The Tortured Poets Department' would be even more piercing in the absence of excess, but instead the clutter lingers, while Swift holds an unlit match.

A few weeks later, the *Times* topped itself by posing the question, 'Will Swift ever voluntarily step away from the spotlight?' – as if beholding a woman in full flow and power invariably summoned the fantasy of her involuntary removal from the scene, just as her profusion had awakened the fantasy of burning parts of it off.

Last time I checked, Swift was not angling to be a great poet; she is a prolific songwriter and performer who gives her fans as much of her music and presence as she can sustain, and has earned a fortune doing so. As an artist, she is clearly, as the late great artist Carolee Schneemann once said about herself, some 'part of nature that just keeps pouring and pouring'. We could simulate incisiveness by deriding this pouring; we could also ask questions about why it summons, for some, the desire to moderate or chasten it, or to fantasise about stopping its flow.

Anne Carson's short essay 'The Gender of Sound' may be instructive here. In it, Carson explains how 'putting a door on the female mouth has been an important project of patriarchal culture from antiquity to the present day'. Carson details how, in ancient Greece, women's sonic outpouring was taken as a threat to the masculine virtue of *sophrosyne*, translated as 'prudence, soundness of mind, moderation, temperance, self-control'. She then links this patriarchal project to more recent incarnations, such as Freud and Breuer's treatment of hysterics in the 1880s, and Ernest Hemingway's panicked response to the largesse of Gertrude Stein's literal voice and body ('[I] tried not to hear any more [of Stein's voice] as I left but it was still going on and the only way I could not hear it was to be gone ... She got to look like a Roman emperor and that was fine if you liked your women to look like Roman emperors'). After describing the many measures that have been put into place to regulate, sequester or eliminate the threat of female 'verbal incontinence' – not to mention the connection, be it implicit or explicit, between the female mouth above and the orifice below – Carson concludes her essay with characteristic understatement: 'Lately I have begun to question the Greek word *sophrosyne* ... I wonder if there might not be another idea of human order than repression, another notion of human virtue than self-control.'

I wonder, too. 'The blood jet is poetry,' Plath wrote. 'There is no stopping it.' Over the course of her short life, Plath's jet included a copious amount of poetry, one novel published and another allegedly destroyed, short stories, letters, journals, children's books and more. Most all of this work was collected and published posthumously; besides *The Colossus*, the only other book Plath published in her lifetime was *The Bell Jar*, and the latter under a pseudonym (Victoria Lucas). Meanwhile, Swift's flow goes on – record-breaking, omnipresent, its own version of unstoppable. In addition to writing (or co-writing) all the songs on her eleven albums (her first released when she was just sixteen), in 2020 Swift

14

embarked on the project of re-recording her first six albums, to regain control of her masters. The re-recorded albums doubled her catalogue, appending a 'Taylor's Version' to each original song. After spending 2023 performing the Eras Tour – the highest-grossing concert tour of all time – in the US, Mexico and South America, Swift added legs in Asia, Europe and Canada, extending the era of Eras for another year; each show is itself an epic, with Swift performing for three and a half hours, singing forty-four songs in ten acts. In 2024, two months after becoming the first artist in history to win a Grammy for Best Album of the Year four times (for 2023's *Midnights*), Swift released the sixteen tracks of *TTPD*. Innumerable fans stayed up late for the midnight drop of *TTPD* (12 a.m. EST, 9 p.m. PST), then struggled to absorb the relatively complicated and dark album in one sitting. A few hours later, in a 2 a.m. EST/11 p.m. PST surprise, Swift dropped an additional fifteen songs, officially flooding the zone. Rather than designate a single from *TTPD* to take the lead, Swift let songs from the album engulf the *Billboard* chart. Within a few weeks, songs from the album occupied all fourteen top spots (another first); the album held the number one spot for three months. In 2024, Swift joined the *Forbes* billionaires list, with *Forbes* reporting that she is the first musician to earn such a sum from songwriting and performing alone, no 'side hustles'.

Given this run, it could be fairly argued that, far from being in danger of suppression, Swift has achieved global domination, and that, in a world increasingly defined and brutalised by inequity, it's only fair to feel antipathy for its biggest winners, especially of the normative (straight, white) variety. But I still think it behoves us to pay attention to how Swift's profusion and power provoke round after round of resentment, animosity, and threat – most obvious in MAGA/incel circles, but elsewhere as well. (Recall Hemingway's distaste for Stein's 'Roman emperor' vibe; now imagine how he might have felt if she had actually been one, rather than just an experimental lesbian writer in an avant-garde demi-monde.)

Swift's artistic flow – and cultural and economic dominance – may feel momentarily overwhelming, but I see no reason not to salute the devotion to living, making, management and survival from which it stems. No one has to like it or listen to it. But it's worth asking what we're doing when we express distaste for female abundance or power; it's worth asking what idea of human order might enable us to celebrate such a phenomenon without the fantasy – or reality – of its castigation, suppression or elimination. After all, women scarcely need reminding that for every record broken, every freedom taken, every bit of power wielded, there is someone out there – perhaps whole armies of them – who would like *very much* to put them back in their place. The overturning of *Roe* v. *Wade* and the feral misogyny of the MAGA movement have made it abundantly clear: this is not a drill.

Hostility to profusion and hostility to the personal are intimately linked, as Carson explains, by a binary-gendered system that values *sophrosyne* overspill: 'Every sound we make is a bit of auto-biography. It has a totally private interior yet its trajectory is public ... The censorship of such projections is a task of patriarchal culture that (as we have seen) divides humanity into two species: those who can censor themselves and those who cannot.' In placing Swift's abundance in opposition to *sophrosyne*, I do not mean to suggest that she (or Plath) lacks self-control. In fact, both could be seen as having extraordinary powers on this account: both evidence a nearly superhuman ability to perform or create under great pressure, albeit of distinct varieties. In both cases, there appears to be a fruitful struggle – recognisable to most artists – between form and flow, superego and id. Plath's poems are – as the *New York Times* critic notes – famously tight (at least in *Ariel*; her earlier poetry and fiction are a bit shaggier). Likewise, it makes no sense to call Swift's songs 'excessive' in and of themselves; most are perfectly orderly pop songs, hovering around four minutes in duration (save one well-known exception, whose title requires not one but two parentheticals: 'All Too Well (10 Minute Version) (Taylor's Version)'). Nor do I mean to suggest that a few grumpy critics dictate the terms of Swift's reception; clearly, they do not. Her fans do, and her fans adore the abundance. For them, there is no such thing as 'too much' – that is, in fact, the fearsome dimension of fandom, its inability to be satisfied. And while critics may chide Swift for a monomaniacal focus on herself and her love life – 'Taylor Swift Needs to Become Other People', fan favourite Ross Douthat opined in the *New York Times*, to the delight of precisely no one – her fans have no problem with it; it is, in fact, a strong part of her allure. Writing songs that people want to hear over and over again is another. ('The bitch can write a hook,' novelist Anna Dorn admits in an essay about moving from Swift-hater to Swift-lover, a transformation that had everything to do with the pleasure of Swift's music: 'I thought my love of [the song] "Delicate" was the exception to the rule: I hate Taylor Swift and everything she represents. But then this summer, after spending three days with a nine-year-old Taylor Swift superfan, I realized my love of "Delicate" *was* the rule: I love Taylor Swift's music.')

The derision of the personal – especially in regard to women – as a politically, aesthetically and ethically rotten source of art is hard to keep track of, as it arrives dressed up in new clothes every decade or so. To consider the most recent history: in the fifties, it was tasteless, inappropriate; in the sixties, it lacked rigour; in the seventies, it was too tied up with identity politics; in the eighties, it was allied with capitalist individualism; in the nineties, it marked the loss of objective truth; in the 2000s, it was neoliberal, and had something to do with the internet; I think the complaint now has to do with reality TV, auto-everything, and the left's failure to collectivise adequately in the face of rising inequity and autocracy – but honestly, it blurs. While critics of varying affiliations carry on with their distaste, readers and listeners everywhere continue to be passionately drawn toward deeply personal work, if only because it tends to make us feel less alone to hear how others experience being a human being.

If and when the accusation of solipsism isn't felt to be ruinous, new portals open. I'm thinking of poet Eileen Myles saying about their work, 'my dirty secret has always been that it's of course about me' – a fun line to place near Swift's 'So tell me everything is not about me / But what if it is?' ('Who's Afraid of Little Old Me?'). There's a big difference between Myles and Swift, in that Swift is speaking from the position of being Somebody in perhaps the most colossal sense possible, whereas Myles is talking about writing out of a sense of being Nobody: 'I have been educated to believe I'm no one so there's a different self operating,' Myles writes. 'You just cannot underestimate the massive difference in writing out of female anonymity.' And yet: through the force and pour of Myles's own writing and career, they are no longer anonymous (nor are they exclusively female): it turns out the binary of Nobody/Somebody – like the gendered binary upon which the regulatory system of *sophrosyne* vs spill rests – is not nearly so fixed (hence, the need to police it).

I have a natural affinity for autobiography. But that doesn't mean I like all art or writing that deploys 'the personal' as a strategy. When I don't like it, however, I usually take it as a sign that the art's no good, which doesn't have much to do with whether it's personal or not. To denigrate the category outright often evidences not only a weird failure to differentiate between the many different strategies, con-texts and effects that have been at play in 'personal' writing for millennia, from Sappho to Montaigne to Keats to Lorde, but also an astonishing literalism, the kind that presumes that work with a disclosing first-person speaker is uncooked confessionalism concerning only a single self, and work without such a thing is not. Nietzsche reminds us otherwise: 'It has gradually become clear to me what every great philosophy up till now has consisted of – namely, the confession of its originator, and a species of involuntary and unconscious autobiography.' We forget this insight at our peril. As Myles once told a *New York Times* reporter, 'You know so much about people from the second they open their mouths. Right away you might know you want to keep them out.' When critics attempt to flex their *sophrosyne* in the face of someone's spill, I usually hear a barely suppressed drive to mastery – to come off as more worldly, more orderly, more contained, more political, more radical, more grown up, more you-name-it. Alongside this stab at superiority, I also often hear a perplexing ingenuousness, wherein the critic's discombobulation at personal content has led them to apprehend a highly crafted pop song or memoir as craft-free discharge. In which case, the joke may be on them – it's a tricky thing, to use artifice to strip artifice of artifice; if and when the critic (or fan) feels that an intimate, unmediated missive has been sent and received, it sometimes just means that the artifice is working.

When women make the personal public, the charge of whorishness always lurks nearby. It doesn't matter much if the artist gets rich or stays broke, because it's not the money that activates the shaming, it's the alleged striptease.

Oddly enough, neither Plath nor Swift is known for being particularly lewd: Plath's close contemporary, Anne Sexton, was far bawdier, and Plath's autobiographical 'exposures' are deeply stylised in symbolism and surrealism (even her most scandalous lines in 'Daddy' – 'Every woman adores a Fascist, / The boot in the face, the brute / Brute heart of a brute like you' – have more to do with power than sex, though I guess it depends on how you roll). Compared with any number of other female pop stars – including Madonna, the sexed-up progenitor of 'blond ambition' – Swift's act is uncommonly clean, at times bordering on chaste. Rather than focus on bodies in all their carnal specificity, Swift's love stories centre on emotions, and her voluminous metaphors for them; even a relatively hot song like 'Guilty as Sin?' figures sex as happening only in the mind: 'These fatal fantasies / Giving way to labored breath / Taking all of me / We've already done it in my head'. But again, it scarcely matters: only a virgin who wants nothing and keeps her wares out of the marketplace can stay pure.

Some people grouse that Swift's artistry is tainted by its being the engine of a billion-dollar industry, and that her creativity cannot be considered apart from her capitalism. Sure – but welcome to the world of pop music; it ain't poetry. (Swift knows this: rather than identify herself solely as the tortured poet, she signs the 'Summary Poem' in the liner notes of *TTPD* 'The Chairman of the Tortured Poets Department', giving vibes more boardroom than Baudelaire.) There is much that poetry and pop music share – a connection to an oral tradition; a kinship between lyric and line; and the capacity to create anthems that can galvanise a public and offer private sustenance, both. But in regard to audience and marketplace, they occupy nearly opposite positions. Pop music is an accessible commodity marketed to the masses that, when successful, can bestow great fame and fortune upon its participants. Poetry's audience, by contrast, is notoriously small. Barring a few exceptions – usually involving work of dubious literary quality – the genre does not sell enough to make its authors rich, or even to pay them at all. Poetry more often *de*values the material it touches: 'a piece of paper with nothing on it has a definite economic value. If you print a poem on it, this value is lost' (poet Charles Bernstein, quoting James Sherry). As a result, poetry occupies both a degraded and exalted place in capitalist culture, insofar as it represents a noble – or idiotic – devotion to an artistic pursuit which, for the most part, repels capital, and compels but a tiny subset of an already small reading public.

Nonetheless, poetry and pop music share a link to the project of fame. Since antiquity, poetry has served as a privileged place from which to praise, memorialise and promote: in short, to make famous, and to grant a form of immortality, however fantasised. In the epic tradition, those made famous are typically political elites, gods and war heroes; in the lyric tradition of love poetry, they are the poet's beloved, and/or the poet himself. I say 'himself' because the posterity project has been primarily, though not exclusively, a patriarchal one, from Homer to Shakespeare to Tennyson: the poem as compensation for death, as vehicle for preserving legacy, as consolation prize for lost or impossible love, as salve for the anxiety of being nobody, or being forgotten – these are preoccupations common to patriarchy, wherein men have been historically granted access to things that women did not have to gain or lose (a name that carries on, war stories, fortunes held in their name, and so on).

Female poets have thus generally had a much weirder relationship to fame. Think, once again, of Dickinson – who is probably, along with Plath, the most famous of female American poets (maybe of all American poets). Dickinson lived a notoriously sequestered life, eventually speaking to others through a door. While alive, she published but ten of the nearly two thousand poems she wrote. From her Amherst outpost, she wrote remarkable lines such as 'Fame is the one that does not stay – / It's [sic] occupant must die'. And this:

Fame is a bee.
It has a song –
It has a sting –
Ah, too, it has a wing.

Fame in Dickinson always appears in a dialectic with obscurity and belatedness – it's as if she knew full well (like Plath) the force of her genius; her secret was that she was keeping that secret from the world, only for it to one day out. (Before she died at age fifty-five, Dickinson asked her sister to burn all of her correspondence, but gave no such instruction for her poems, which she left in her room, more or less ready to be found – not that she could have foretold their wing.)

The past sixty years have seen radical changes in the public positions available to women in lyric:

think Anna Akhmatova, Gwendolyn Brooks, Joy Harjo, Adrienne Rich, Audre Lorde, Nikki Giovanni and more. But despite poetry's communal rituals (the open mic, the reading series, ritualised inclusion at weddings, funerals and inaugurations), it remains mostly a private sport, written and read by people in their solitude. Not only that, but even household names like Plath and Dickinson are famous primarily for being famous poets – I doubt that many who know of them have actually read them. Most probably know only that Dickinson was a shut-in; Plath, a suicide. Pop music, on the other hand, is called pop because it's popular. People can enjoy it alone, but they – we – tend to enjoy it together, at dance parties, listening parties, live shows, the gym, skating rinks, or just driving around, singing in unison. Due to its reach, the benchmarks for its success lie in aggregate numbers: streams on Spotify, stadium capacity, radio plays, cities visited, LPs sold, Grammys won, profits grossed.

Yet even with this vast audience, pop music is still not thought of as a vehicle for lasting fame in the way that poetry is. The medium is not nearly as old, of course, and the technology for recorded music isn't that much older. But it may be that the bad rap poetry receives for its esoteric nature factors into its grip. While poetry can be a young person's game (think Rimbaud, Keats, Plath), it is also (thankfully!) one for the ageing and old. It does not rely on a singer capable of performing for three and a half hours in compression hose and a sequin onesie. Rather, it consists of words that may or may not be confined to the page. These words can be rendered material in a variety of ways – memory, manuscript, typewriter, screen, voice memo, Braille reader, etc. – no phonograph or streaming app required. Plus, poetry's historical relationship to hardship – of both the psychic and economic variety – only burnishes its reputation as an authentic, perhaps *the* most authentic, form of artistic expression. In fact, I can scarcely think of a group of people more inclined toward grandiosity than poets: with so little earthly reward, you need exceptionally strong drive and a measure of perversity to commit your life to the genre. (Think of this exchange from *The Bell Jar*, in which a photographer for *Ladies' Day* magazine asks our anti-hero what she wants to be: '"She wants," said [my boss] wittily, "to be everything." I said I wanted to be a poet.')

The written word's claim on immortality and authenticity is likely why Swift, along with many other musicians, leans into its tropes when she wants a figure for something less evanescent than a song (as in Swift's short film for 'All Too Well', in which our female lead suffers a painful love affair, then emerges at a bookstore to sign copies of *All Too Well*, the book she presumably wrested from the debacle. See also *TTPD*'s bonus song 'The Manuscript', in which Swift sings, 'The only thing that's left is the manuscript / One last souvenir from my trip to your shores'). The idea of the manuscript as lasting souvenir from an unconsummated or unrecoverable love hearkens back to one of Western poetry's origin stories: in Greek myth, the god Apollo – the god of poetry – is consumed with lust for virginal river nymph Daphne; Daphne runs from him, praying to her river god father to turn her into a laurel tree to evade Apollo's advances. After her father turns Daphne into a tree, Apollo picks its laurel leaves to signify a consolation prize for his failed rape: hence, the poet laureate is born.

It's interesting to think about Swift's pouring and power in relation to this narrative: rather than a mute, motionless, virginal Daphne, we get a hyper-productive, globetrotting, serial dater who tells us, 'I could go on and on, on and on – and I will' ('This Love'). The serial dating, whether or not it continues in IRL, has been crucial to Swift's work, as it has turned a series of men ('all the Kens', in her parlance) into footnotes to her career, rather than vice versa.

It's this going on and on in increments of song – and album – that has led to one of Swift's greatest innovations: the Eras Tour, which cannily merges lyric and epic traditions, transforming both by rooting them in girlhood and womanhood. The Eras Tour is truly a 'feminine epic', as theorised by poet Alice Notley back in the 1990s. When Notley set herself the task of writing such a thing (which she eventually achieved, in *The Descent of Alette*), she says she immediately found herself faced with the problem of 'what do women *do*', when so often their role is, in Notley's words, 'essentially passive: sufferer, survivor'. After much experimentation, Notley found her answer in dreams (in which, she says, women 'participate in stories every night of their lives'); Swift found her answer in feelings, and in songs that hold their stories. Nearly all but a handful of the forty-four songs on Swift's Eras set list are in the lyric tradition of love poetry: a first-person speaker addresses either a 'you' or a 'he', and gives an account of her feelings over the course of their love, their failed love, or both. Yet the show itself – in duration, production value, audience size, global reach, and economic effect on the cities and countries through which it passes – is absolutely epic.

More epic still is its foundational concept: it's a heroine's journey – not through a war, or a trip back from war, or the underworld, or the founding of a city, but through the stations of the cross of Swift's emotional and artistic life, from girlhood to present day, signified by different 'eras', each with their own colour scheme, stage set, costuming and song list. (In furtherance of her manuscript chic, Swift's outfit for the new *TTPD* era set is a white Vivienne Westwood dress printed with calligraphic writing, as if she herself has become the manuscript.) Swift is not out to subvert femininity, but it's crucial that the eras are not defined by stations of life stereotypically associated with girlhood or womanhood, such as maiden, wife, mother, and so on. Instead they are defined by *artistic achievement*, represented by the unit of the album. Thus, the eras do not unfold in chronological order, but rather in the order Swift wants them to appear for the purposes of the show. *This* is the radical takeaway for legions of her young fans: the story of your life is literally what your art makes of it.

In a 2012 interview with *Vogue*, when asked whether she was ever freaked out by her fame (which is, ironically, exponentially greater now than it was then), Swift responded: 'This is what I've wanted to do my whole life. It never freaks me out. Never. Ever. But you know what does freak me out? When is the other shoe going to drop? I am so happy right now. So I am always living in fear. This can't be real, right? This can't really be my life.' I don't typically take what people say to interviewers at face value, but I'm nonetheless riveted by *It never freaks me out. Never. Ever.* I'm riveted by it because it points to one of the rarest things about Swift, which is how good she is at being famous, which may have to do in part with how clearly she owns her lifelong desire for it.

I personally enjoy hearing Swift – and other very famous people – talk about the travails of being famous, but I have come to recognise that I am in a minority here. I think the problem is twofold: one, great fame is a rarified experience, so few people can relate to it; and two, people generally feel that fame and fortune are so awesome, why would anyone complain about achieving them, and why would we want to listen to someone's sob story about being on top of the world? I get it (kind of). But there's another dimension to all this when it comes to women, which is that hearing about fame from a woman in a position of obscurity (like Dickinson) may feel more tolerable than hearing about it from someone living through it (like Swift) or desperately desiring it (like Plath). I think, here, of Dickinson's weird little poem about being Nobody vs being Somebody:

I'm Nobody! Who are you?
Are you – Nobody – too?
Then there's a pair of us!
Don't tell! they'd advertise – you know!

How dreary – to be – Somebody!
How public – like a Frog –
To tell one's name – the livelong June –
To an admiring Bog!

It's almost as if Dickinson is trying to convince herself that it would be unspeakably dreary – not just dreary, but tawdry, slimy – to try to become Somebody. No doubt, there weren't many ways of becoming Somebody on offer to a female poet in nineteenth-century New England. But just as a thought experiment, imagine that, instead of writing out of 'the massive difference ... of female anonymity', Dickinson had chased and achieved the stature she's come to have. How would she have borne the refrigerator magnets, the tote bags, the Apple TV series, the mugs, the memes, the T-shirts, the tattoos, the valuation, the mockery? Easier to disdain the whole 'admiring bog', and remain unstained by the degradations of being 'advertised'.

Plath took a different tack. Despite her posthumous fame as a representative of 'high art', while she was alive, Plath wanted literary success on a mass level. She was, as Rose says, 'shameless in her desire to write for this market', and sent her writing to *Mademoiselle*, *Ladies' Home Journal*, the *New Yorker*, the *Saturday Evening Post*, *McCall's*, *Good Housekeeping*, *Women's Day* and *Seventeen*. As Plath put it, in terms the young Swift would likely have understood (and that would likely have appalled Dickinson): 'I will slave and slave until I break into those slicks.' Plath may have been a snob about some things (I have no doubt she was; magnanimity was not her calling card), but, as Rose details, her ambition overpowered any snobbery about venue. What's more, unlike many female artists who attempt to prove their seriousness by avoiding platforms that cater to women or teens, Plath went for both full throttle.

The Bell Jar is remarkable in that it aimed for (and eventually achieved) this mass appeal while also insisting on explosive, taboo-busting content, especially for its time. But Plath never saw the book published under her name – she used a pseudonym in part for legal reasons, and in part because her confidence in the book had been shaken: Harper & Row, the publisher that had initially funded the project, declined to publish after reading it, finding it 'disappointing, juvenile and overwrought'. Plath had to scramble to find a different publisher, and when the book came out in January 1963, it garnered only a handful of tepid reviews. Plath took her life four weeks later. It wasn't until 1966 that the novel appeared under her name, and became the kind of cultural sensation – including becoming a staple of high school curricula for decades – that she had dreamt about.

Like the figure of Plath herself, *The Bell Jar* continues to ricochet between adulation and devaluation, while having sold over three million copies and counting. (I can imagine Swift knows the feeling. 'Anything I do is polarizing,' she good-naturedly tells a *New York Times* reporter. 'So, you know, I'm used to that.') This is part of how fame works: it replaces a human being with a figure upon which innumerable others play out a sometimes ferocious drama of assessment and valuation. For the famous person, this often occasions a splitting, by which the original subject (and the name it goes by) must protect itself by undergoing a sort of death, from which it must emerge reborn. As Swift puts it in 'Look What You Made Me Do': 'I'm sorry, the old Taylor can't come to the phone right now. / Why? 'Cause she's dead.' The famous person learns – or struggles to learn, or never learns – how to inhabit this name while garnering some distance from it. ('I have found a way to live to the side of my name,' says political philosopher Judith Butler, whose name now travels the globe as a signifier for the celebrated and demonised concept of 'gender ideology', exposing Butler to great esteem and threat.) The trick is to carry on as the human being she still is even as she has come to signify a phenomenon that exceeds

45

her – sometimes vastly – and over which she has little control.

As any reader of *Ariel* knows, Plath's late poetry is saturated with figures of death and rebirth. They are not bejewelled. In addition to the burnt-up speaker of 'Lady Lazarus', there's the reborn amnesiac of 'Getting There', who concludes: 'And I, stepping from this skin / Of old bandages, boredoms, old faces / Step up to you from the black car of Lethe, / Pure as a baby.' Swift plays with no such high stakes (though her toothless wraith made mean by 'the circus life' in 'Who's Afraid of Little Old Me?' is a surprising step in Plath's direction). She does, however, alight on the relationship between death, fame and femininity. The most haunting instance is 'Clara Bow', the last track on *TTPD* (before the bonus record!), whose lyrics shift back and forth between the voices of an aspiring starlet and the industry executives who act as her judge and gatekeeper. In the voice of the starlet, Swift sings, 'I'm not trying to exaggerate / But I think I might die if it happened / Die if it happened to me'; the lyric later returns: 'I'm not trying to exaggerate / But I think I might die if I made it / Die if I made it.'

The first time I heard this song, I felt immeasurably sad. I think it was the repetition of the word 'die' that did it: even if 'I think I might die' is just a figure of speech signifying overexcitement – the way we desire, and fear, being overwhelmed by the actualisation of our wildest dreams – it also holds within it the evaporation of the ambitious woman right at the moment of her achievement (not unlike Plath, whose death 'made her' and annihilated her at once). More worrisome still is the dread that 'making it' – even if intensely desired and achieved – holds

47

within it multiple deaths, not just of the old, pre-fame self, but also of the new, famous self, once the other shoe drops, and the world's attention has moved on. *I am always living in fear. This can't be real, right?* When Swift sings her own name in 'Clara Bow', in the voice of an executive comparing the aspiring star in front of him with the once-famous singer ('You look like Taylor Swift / In this light, we're loving it'), that's the weird chime we hear – the sound of the living who knows that one day her moment will pass, that one day her name, too, will join those of the dead. *Fame is the one that does not stay / It's occupant must die.* Nothing lasts forever; at some point, even the bounty of Swift's songs will no longer seem like enough. People will rue that the pouring is over; the wish to 'burn away all the peripherals' will be replaced by a scouring of the archive, just as Plath's archive has been the subject of intense revisitation for decades now, with no sign of letting up. Or, maybe not – no one can be sure what will become of their legacy once they're gone, and no one lives to find out.

'Clara Bow' doesn't make me sad any more. It doesn't make me sad because, as it becomes an earworm, as so many of Swift's songs do, it transforms, and exceeds the sum of its lyrical parts. It means differently depending on whether you're walking with earbuds, sitting on the subway, cooking dinner, or making friendship bracelets with children who don't have a clue who or what Swift is talking about, and don't really care. After all, trying to stay on top in an industry that has female obsolescence baked into its DNA, or grappling with the perils of being an 'It girl' (as was Clara Bow's nickname), are not widely shared dilemmas. But pop songs become popular because listeners fill in the blanks with their own preoccupations; they are not a one-way signal. When I listen to 'Clara Bow' now, I think about Swift's dilemma, but I also think about how all our abundance, all our clutter, all our names, will eventually rejoin the earth's debris. I think about the fear, excitement and pathos of wanting something badly, no matter its unknowns, no matter the untold transformations it may bring; I think about the impermanence that attenuates all our bids for singularity and survival. I respect that 'Clara Bow' gives us all that, while also giving us something fun to mouth.

Back in 2014, Swift told *Time*, 'I see a lot of celebrities build up these emotional walls around themselves, where they let no one in, and that's what makes them feel very lonely at the top.

I just keep writing songs. And I kind of stay open to feeling humiliated and rejected, because before being a quote-unquote celebrity, I'm a songwriter. Being a celebrity means you lock your doors and close your windows and don't let people in. Being a songwriter means you're very attuned to your own intuition and your own feelings even if they hurt.' Artists have to open themselves – often radically – to *something* in order to create. *What* they open to – their hurt feelings, a formal idea, political convictions, divine visitation, a philosophical question, the pleasures of a medium – may matter less than the fact of the opening itself. I have no idea how hard it has been for Swift to manage this negotiation between closing and opening over the years, but from the outside a decade on, it sure looks like it's working pretty well. And while Swift is here talking about the particular challenge that celebrity poses to art-making, the fact is that anyone who puts their work into the world, at any level, must learn to navigate between self-protectiveness and risk, becoming harder and staying soft. It's not quite the same as Buddhist Pema Chödrön's meditation on learning to be 'big and small at the same time', but it feels related:

> I was once invited to teach with the Sakyong Mipham Rinpoche, my teacher's eldest son, in a situation where it wasn't exactly clear what my status was. Sometimes I was treated as a big deal who should come in through a special door and sit in a special seat. Then I'd think, 'Okay, I'm a big deal.' I'd start running with that idea and come up with big-deal notions about how things should be. Then I'd get the message, 'Oh, no, no, no. You should just sit on the floor and mix with everybody and be one of the crowd.' Okay. So now the

message was that I should just be ordinary, not set myself up or be the teacher. But as soon as I was getting comfortable with being humble, I would be asked to do something special that only big deals did. This was a painful experience because I was always being insulted and humiliated by my own expectations. As soon as I was sure how it should be, so I could feel secure, I would get a message that it should be the other way. Finally I said to the Sakyong, 'This is really hurting. I just don't know who I'm supposed to be,' and he said, 'Well, you have to learn to be big and small at the same time.'

Learning to bounce between feeling humiliated and feeling secure, feeling powerful and feeling powerless, is no small charge, be it in art or in life. I think, once again, of Plath's 'The Colossus', wherein Plath's Lilliputian speaker 'crawl[s] like an ant in mourning / Over the weedy acres of [the statue's] brow', squats in the statue's ear while 'Counting the red stars and those of plum-color', then picnics on a nearby hill of black cypress. Not unlike Swift, whose songs often pay homage to a male beloved, Plath often imagines herself in thrall to – and/or crushed by – a male beloved, father or god. It's easy to discount this trope as retrograde, as in some sense, it is. It's also a time-worn way for women to play with power – the pleasure of having it, giving it up, being beside it, stealing it, and sometimes – as has been possible for Swift in ways that were not on the menu for Plath – possessing and wielding it at an unprecedented scale.

Despite her fantasies of being a 'girl who wanted to be God', or rising up from the dead to 'eat men like air', Plath did not die in a position of power. She died sick and struggling, the distressed mother of two young children, in the middle of a severe depressive episode she fought but did not beat. As an educated, middle-class white woman, Plath had a measure of privilege. But she struggled to afford much-needed psychiatric care, and for periods of her life had to rely on the generosity of an older writer and philanthropist – Olive Higgins Prouty – to fund her hospitalisation and treatment. (Some Plath scholars think her guilt at how much her medical care was costing her mother factored into Plath's 1953 suicide attempt; after the attempt, Prouty stepped in to pay for Plath to be institutionalised at a private psychiatric hospital, McLean). Plath's final depression saw her frantically sending out poems for pay (an oxymoron now, but then, a source of marginal income), and opting to stay in England – where she was fairly isolated – in part due to the free healthcare. As Anne Thériault notes in a 2017 article about Plath and the NHS, in her last letter to her mother, Plath explained: 'I could never afford to live in America. I get the best of doctors' care here perfectly free, and with the children this is a great blessing ... I shall simply have to fight it out on my own over here.' She took her life a week later, while on the waitlist for a bed in a psychiatric ward.

One of the most haunting and galling passages I've ever read on Plath (and I've read a lot) comes from her friend A. Alvarez's account of visiting her in the weeks leading up to her death. Alvarez writes: 'She called me on Christmas Eve: would I like to come and see the new flat, eat a meal, hear some poems? I said I'd drop by. I hardly recognised Sylvia when she opened the door. The bright young American house wife with her determined smile and crisp clothes had vanished along with the pancake make-up, the school-mistressy bun and fake cheerfulness. Her face was wax-pale and drained: her hair hung loose down to her waist and left a faint, sharp animal scent on the air when she walked ahead of me up the stairs. She looked like a priestess emptied out by the rites of her cult.' What galls me is the swift movement from noting all the hallmarks of a dangerous depression (failing hygiene, etc.) to a mythological fantasia in which Plath becomes forlorn priestess rather than human being in dire need. This is the deadly and perverse mechanism of 'making famous': it moves someone from human to myth right in front of our eyes. (The chapter on Plath in Alvarez's 1971 book, *The Savage God: A Study of Suicide*, played a pivotal role in this reputational conversion.) To borrow a phrase from Plath's 'Lady Lazarus', *Beware, beware* – not necessarily of the vengeful ghost of a wronged, silver-tongued woman, but of how we ourselves risk dehumanising others without even noticing what we're up to, or in spite of our best intentions.

To be fair, Alvarez had his regrets: in the same piece, he writes: 'I left knowing I had let her down unforgivably. I told myself she was Ted's responsibility and Ted was my friend. But that wasn't the whole story. I wasn't up to her despair and it scared me. Seven weeks later she committed suicide.' Perhaps Alvarez makes his move toward myth in an effort to offload guilt – after all, a forlorn priestess emptied out of the rites of her cult is a lot harder to reach than a broke mom with bad-smelling hair in the throes of a mental health crisis. Not that I blame him: Alvarez had his own demons, and who can say what would have helped. What's done is done – to the extent that Plath's story is ever done. (Clearly, for me, it's not.)

To be more fair still: Plath was an active participant in her self-mythologisation, and not
just in her poems. Whether this propensity
is a condition of possibility for a certain level
of ambition and fame, I leave undecided. But
there is no doubt that one of the most compelling and frightening aspects of her relationship
with Hughes had to do with the collision of
two powerful, even dangerous people, both prone
to mythologising not just themselves, but their
union and dissolution – likely to no good end for
anyone within their blast radius. (I find Hughes's
later-in-life poetry about Plath unreadable for
this reason; Swift apparently does not, as she
posted the Hughes poem 'Red' shortly after the
release of *TTPD* – though, for whatever reason,
took it down soon after.) In the face of Hughes
and Plath's disastrous collision, the chorus of the
title song 'The Tortured Poets Department' feels
like dopey reprieve, as when Swift tells her lover,

'You're not Dylan Thomas, I'm not Patti Smith / This ain't the Chelsea Hotel, we're modern idiots.' It's corny, for sure, but its capacity for deflation also feels potentially life-saving. To feel idiot means that one hasn't forgotten how to be small – and by 'small', I don't necessarily mean insulted or humiliated (feelings which can – and have, in both Plath and Swift – lend themselves to aggrandisement). I just mean 'small' as in living a life with no more or less insight into what it's all about than anyone else's, and with no more or less inherent value.

Plath was but seventeen years old when she wrote the line about 'the girl who wanted to be God'. The line is well known; less well known is the larger context in her journal from which it comes: 'I am afraid of getting older. I am afraid of getting married. Spare me from cooking three meals a day—spare me from the relentless cage of routine and rote. I want to be free ... I want, I think, to be omniscient ... I think I would like to call myself "The girl who wanted to be God." Yet if I were not in this body, where *would* I be—perhaps I am destined to be classified and qualified. But, oh, I cry out against it. I am I—I am powerful—but to what extent? I am I.' Everywhere in Plath's work we can feel this drive toward freedom, toward power, and a rage against the conditions that inhibited it, including those within herself. Swift's work stages related protests – we're not out of the woods yet, and fame obviously constructs its own special cage. But insofar as Swift has claimed, or created, an enormous space to find out just how powerful she is, as an artist, economic force and element of nature, she has rearranged the scene.

Late in the Eras show, Swift sings 'Midnight Rain', a hymn to her ambition and where it's taken her. The song contrasts Swift's drive and darkness to the placidity and light of a male lover from her youth: 'He was sunshine, I was midnight rain / He wanted it comfortable, I wanted that pain / He wanted a bride, I was making my own name / Chasing that fame, he stayed the same / All of me changed like midnight rain.' As Swift sings about 'the life [she] gave away', she struts down the runway in Christian Louboutin glitter boots and an Oscar de la Renta bodysuit adrip with sapphire beads, her male dancer of the stunning abs spinning an umbrella deferentially by her side. I rejoice at the spectacle, and also can't help thinking of Plath, as a kind of flipside of the coin: Plath's face wax-pale and drained, hair unwashed and loose, opening the door to let Alvarez into her flat. When Swift sings 'he was sunshine / I was midnight rain', I hear Plath excoriating her mother, 'Don't talk to me about the world needing cheerful stuff.' When

Swift sings 'making my own name, chasing my fame', I hear Plath's furious vow, 'I will slave and slave until I break into those slicks.' When Swift sings 'All of me changed like midnight rain,' I hear her and Plath's conjoined commitment to transformation, to going wherever their pour might take them. 'Every sound we make is a bit of autobiography,' Carson tells us. Let it rain.

Thank you: Fern Press, PJ Mark, Michelle Tea, Brooke Palmieri, Beth Pickens, Harry Dodge, Sophia Stid, Ben Lerner, Brian Blanchfield, Carrie Hansen, Emily Nelson, Ian Whceler-Nicholson, Darcy Wheeler and Iggy Dodge-Nelson.